WESTERN EUROPE

Leslie Gardiner

FAMILY LIBRARY
of
WORLD TRAVEL

First published in 1985
for AGT Publishing
by Octopus Books Limited
59 Grosvenor Street
London W1, England

© 1985 Octopus Books Limited

ISBN 0–933521–16–2

Produced by Mandarin Publishers Ltd
22a Westlands Road
Quarry Bay, Hong Kong

Jacket Photography: Zefa Picture Library

The tower that Paris learned to live with *previous page*. Gustav Eiffel's tower was a fairground novelty, focal point of the Grand Exposition of 1889. When Marconi's wireless telegraph came, the 985-foot folly had its uses: it became a transmitter. It stands in the city's heart, astride the Champ de Mars. Its three platforms, accessible by elevator, have restaurants and snack bars.

Majestic sweep of the German Rhine *this page*. 'The Rhine is always the Rhine' – German proverb. But horseshoe bends and ox-bow lakes show how its meandering course has changed through the ages. The river is both the busiest industrial artery and the principal scenic waterway of Europe.

CONTENTS

INTRODUCTION

From northern Norway to southern Spain is a long haul – the equivalent in latitude to a journey from North Alaska to North Carolina. The climate ranges from Arctic frost (tempered by warm offshore currents) to sub-tropical heat (likewise moderated by the sea). The social spectrum is equally broad, from primitive shepherds and fishermen to captains of industry and the sun-seeking jet set.

Three of our featured countries, France, Germany and Switzerland, have been tourist centers for centuries. France reveals Renaissance palaces and formal gardens, teaches us a love of food and opens our eyes to a more light-hearted, relaxed outlook on life. Germany introduces us to medieval showplaces, frowning fortresses, comic-opera princelings, to great music, libraries, colleges and renowned philosophers and scientists. In Switzerland we can enjoy breath-taking mountain scenery, bright, clean towns and the most delicious chocolate. That is, when we are not sunning ourselves on the golden beaches of the Côte d'Azur, walking in the Black Forest or skiing in the Swiss Alps.

Spain looks a little out of place on the map of Europe. History tells of a country which, having had its century of fame and glory, gave up the struggle and went to sleep. Modern tourism has discovered enchanting old cities embedded in Spain's mountainous heart. More dramatically, Spain's neglected coastline has become a golden chain of vacation resorts which, in the space of two or three decades, have established themselves as the most popular destinations in Europe.

Denmark also is fast coming forward as a major tourist attraction. It has all the qualifications: a capital city famed for good cooking and the joy of living, a riviera coastline, 1000 miles of soft sand beaches, countless little islands to tempt the lover of solitude, old forts and manor houses ... most important of all, perhaps, an enlightened and efficient attitude to tourism and a high standard of cleanliness.

Cleanliness and neatness are also features of Norway and Sweden, as are a reputation for a rich and imaginative cuisine. Fjord cruises in Norway, with the *aurora borealis* an added attraction, have long been among the world's great tourist experiences. Norway invented winter sports and in its mountainland skiing is both a sport and a way of life.

Sweden, a land designed by nature for curious visitors, has never known mass tourism. A remarkable mixture of scenic wilderness and sophisticated engineering, Sweden has harnessed natural resources with canals, for example, which penetrate a wild and wonderful landscape. Now we can travel on them, and explore the wilderness in comfort – or rough it, if we prefer, on long-distance hunting and camping trips. And an archipelago of delightful islands is available to visitors too.

Aurlandsfjord: the silence and majesty of Nature undisturbed *left.* Since the continents took their shape and plants appeared on the land, perhaps 400 million years ago, the northern fjords of Scandinavia have looked like this. Most Scandinavians live within ten miles of the sea; the harvest of the sea has been their lifeblood. But the fjords are many and in at least some no fish are taken, no tree is cut down and no exploitation of minerals is attempted. When the cruise ship ruffles the water of a fjord such as this, passengers look on nature in its inviolate majesty.

SPAIN

Madrid • Toledo • Castile
Segovia • Seville • Granada
Mallorca • Costa Brava • Cerdana

Sabbrena: ancient fortress village.
'The villages are the heart of Spain,'
said John dos Passos. Superficial
changes have brightened villagers'
lives – bathrooms, ice-boxes,
automobiles – but they still hold to the
patriarchal traditions of the
countryside and their everyday
routine may be much the same as
that of their distant forebears.

Even to other Europeans, Spain is an exotic land, sealed off beyond the snowy Pyrenees. It has developed separately – lagged behind in some ways – and has preserved in its isolation some customs and pastimes (bullfighting, for instance) which most Europeans find strange.

Much of Spain is harsh mountainland, parched in summer, icy in winter, split by fantastic gorges up which crawl the dusty, tormented roads. The colored peaks, topped with fortresses and monasteries, seemed inaccessible to early travelers. Air travel has changed all that. Europe learned that the mountainland stopped short on an azure sea and in places stood back to provide a dramatic skyline for glamorous beaches. In three short decades long ribbons of coastline have been transformed. New names – Costa Brava, Costa Blanca, Costa del Sol – have appeared on the map, and foreigners have flocked in to enjoy the golden beaches, blue skies and warm seas; and to sample the abundant food and cheap but good wine that make the perfect seaside holiday.

Confused and exhausted after days among the relics of antiquity, the Mediterranean traveler greets Madrid with relief: not an ancient monument in sight! Up to 300 years ago, Madrid was an insignificant market town. But in this highest capital city of Europe, the mathematical center of Spain, there is no lack of things to see and do. Madrid is a fine place for strolling. The principal park, the Retiro, has woodland and lakes and entertainments. Some plazas (city squares) are pedestrianized, notably the Plaza Mayor, and bordered with small taverns and shops of country character. A stroll down the Calle Mayor ends in a district of bars with guitarists and accordionists.

The heavily baroque Royal Palace, dating from the early 1700s, is now a nest of museums. (King Juan Carlos lives at Zarzuela, outside the city.) Opposite, under an enormous dome, stands the 19th-century cathedral of San Francisco el Grande, a landmark for miles around. On a third side of the esplanade, the Campo del Moro, the National Coach Museum, exhibits ornate carriages of old Spain. The Manzanare, Madrid's insignificant river, trickles beneath.

The prized attraction is the Prado, near the Retiro park. One of the world's major picture galleries, it is the only place for a proper study of that line of idiosyncratic Spanish painters which begins with Velasquez and El Greco and ends with Picasso and Dali.

The city is hot and dusty in summer. Half its population makes for

The Alcala Gate, a stone frame for downtown Madrid *right.* Sabatini's city gate built in 1778 bestrides the old exit from Madrid to eastern Spain. It looks down the Calle de Alcala to the busy intersection of Plaza de Cibeles. 'Great mother' of Asiatic myth, honored in Greece and Rome, Cybele is represented in Plaza de Cibeles as a goddess in a chariot, drawn by two lions amid splashing fountains – a piece of sculpture loved by Madrileños and a trademark of the city. On the Plaza (left side) are the Bank of Spain and the ecclesiastical-looking General Post Office.

Toledo, city of swordsmiths and painters *right*. Caught in a loop of the Tagus river, the living museum of Toledo – six centuries Moorish, five centuries Spanish – climbs up its rock. The grandiose cathedral (1227–1493), part Gothic and part Renaissance, has five naves, innumerable chapels and 84 massive columns. Riverbank streets in the foreground lead to the four-square Moorish Alcazar, pictured here. This palace-fortress, associated with El Cid the national hero, was destroyed in the Civil War of 1936–39 and since rebuilt. The house of El Greco, son of Toledo, is among other 16th-century houses on the right of our picture.

Burgos, where the best Spanish is spoken *left*. Courses in Spanish for foreigners are held at Burgos in northern Castile. The pure Castilian tongue is spoken there. The fretted spires of Burgos cathedral, shown here, are visible many miles away. The building was begun in 1221 but the towers and facade belong to Spanish Gothic's best period, the early 14th century. This is the third largest cathedral in Spain, after those of Seville and Toledo. General Franco heard mass here in July 1936, before being appointed *caudillo* (military dictator) of Nationalist Spain. An earlier warrior-chief, El Cid, whose name crops up everywhere in these parts, is buried beside his wife in the cathedral transept.

the coast. Winters are cool, with rain. Spring is delightfully flowery and autumn splendid with all the woodland in full color.

The favorite excursion from Madrid is to the Escorial. It is 30 miles to the northwest and is a rather bleak monastery, the biggest granite building in the world. The kings and queens of Spain are buried there.

From Irun on the French frontier, 400 miles of tree-lined coast – pines, cypresses and groves of citrus fruits – run due west. The first section, the Basque country around the beaches of San Sebastian, is fun for day-tourists from France but it is not the real Spain. In fact, separatist Basques stridently argue that it is not Spain at all. That mysterious race, with its own unusual language, probably descends from aboriginals whom the Spanish Celts almost wiped out.

Both San Sebastian and Santander are pleasant resorts for a stay-put family holiday. Bilbao, between the two, is an industrial blot on the landscape. Founded in the 13th century, Bilbao is considered one of Spain's modern cities.

In the far west, towards the fortress walls and cobbled streets of La Coruna and the fishing port of Vigo which is barricaded with islets, the coast is steep and deeply indented.

The unusual features of this Biscayan coast should not be missed. Guernica, near Bilbao, symbolizes the horrors of a modern civil war, thanks to the Picasso painting (which hangs in the Museum of Modern Art, New York). The caves of Altamira, first stumbled upon in 1881, contain brilliant paintings by early artists of *c.* 10,000 BC,

Segovia's stone prow rides the high Sierra *above*. The Alcazar of Segovia, like an old-fashioned battleship, rises to meet the waves and has the cathedral (on the left) in tow. This 14th-century Moorish palace was damaged by fire last century and restoration, for better or worse, emphasized the idea of the unattainable 'castles in Spain.' The cathedral, with marble statuary, a ceramic altar and rare Flemish tapestries, was completed around 1600 and was the last major Gothic work in Spain. A walkway along the city walls, from the Alcazar to the almost-intact Roman aqueduct half a mile away, displays fine cameos of Segovia's crowded houses and neat Romanesque churches.

but the very best caves are visitable only with prior permission. The third unique sight is the sacred city of Santiago de Compostela, between La Coruna and Vigo. Sant' Iago (St. James the Apostle) is the patron of Spain. The town is a theater of ecclesiastical splendor and Iago's tomb is the goal of international pilgrims.

From this remote district of Finisterre ('Land's End'), the well-engineered up-hill-and-down-dale roads, lightly trafficked, struggle towards the interior. They enter Castile, land of castles. Most tourists are 'just passing through' – a pity, because many towns deserve detailed inspection. If time is limited, visit at least Valladolid, to see the houses where Cervantes lived and Columbus died, and Salamanca, in gleaming golden sandstone above a destructive torrent, with no fewer than three old universities. Also visit rockbound Segovia, 3000 feet above sea level, with its Alcazar (fortified palace) and a well-preserved Roman aqueduct, and Toledo, of incalculable age, 11th-century stronghold of the national hero El Cid and metropolis of the armaments trade when swordsmanship was in fashion.

The 'Snowy Sierra' of Spain's hot south *above*. Stifled under apéritif umbrellas or broiling on hotel terraces of the Costa del Sol, tourists can see the cool peaks of the Sierra Nevada or 'Snowy Range.' It is well named. The upper ridges, visible only from far out to sea, wear their dust coats of snow all the year round. High-level winter sports resorts are spreading over the shoulders of the mountains, which reach their greatest altitude in Mulhacén (11,420 feet), the highest peak in Spain.

The cornfields and rich red earth of New Castile merge into Andalucia, a country of sun-baked landscapes and dazzling white towns. (Europe's all-time highest temperature, 124 F or 41 C, was recorded at Seville in this province.) The narrow streets, high walls, minarets and wrought-iron balconies of Andalucia's towns proclaim the influence of Islam. Only in 1492, the year Columbus discovered America, did Spain finally drive out the Moors.

South of Toledo, near Ciudad Real, signposted routes trace the wanderings of Don Quixote through La Mancha, Toboso and other scenes of the doleful knight's adventures. Cordoba venerates Don Quixote's inn, but is more celebrated for the alabaster courts of La Mezquita and the Moorish cathedral, the Juderia ghetto with 14th-century synagogue, and the lovely gardens of the Alcazar along the rippling Guadalquivir river.

Towards Les Marismas, where the Guadalquivir loiters in the marshes, our route arrives at Seville, a gorgeous array of mosques, Alcazar, patios and arabesqued towers. Christopher Columbus's bones lie under the cathedral, which was once a mosque and is now the world's largest church outside Rome. Seville is full of color and vitality except on Holy Friday (Easter) when the processions of

The hanging houses of Cuenca
below. Halfway house on the road from Madrid to Valencia, the small town of Cuenca gives its name to a province and occupies an escarpment of rock above the stony valley of the River Júcar. The oldest parts of the town, which go back 800 years and more, are an urban curiosity. Some of the dwellings are plastered against the rock face, with ladder-like rock-cut steps for exits and entrances. Mothers chain their babies to the jutting balconies to stop them from crawling into empty space. Spain's only museum of abstract art is located among the 'hanging houses.'

Granada: terracotta citadel of the caliphs *above.* The fabulous complex of the Alhambra – courts, ramparts, watch-towers, palace, seraglio, columns and arches – is built of red clay bricks; its oldest part, the alcazabar or citadel, has survived for 1100 years. Its history touches the history of Spain at many points, up to the year 1492 when it was surrendered to King Ferdinand and Queen Isabella. (Their tombs are in Granada at the foot of the hill.) The Alhambra was afterwards desecrated, abandoned and magnificently restored.

Stately riverscape of old Seville *left.* The cupola of the Torre del Oro ('Golden Tower') gleams like the lantern of a rococo lighthouse over Seville's waterways and the Plaza de España, shown here. Along the Guadalquivir close by, the esplanades begin, skirting the palm- and tangerine-fringed walks of the Delicias and Maria Luisa parks, favored venues of the citizens for their evening promenades.

hooded penitents shuffle through the streets to sorrowful music. Holy days, solemn and cheerful, are celebrated throughout Spain with extravagant fairs and festivals.

Beside the 60-mile-wide Guadalquivir delta, Cadiz occupies a narrow neck of land. It could be a town of Morocco: lime-washed houses, date palms, a market piled high with oranges. It is the harbor for Jerez and the vineyards of white grapes which produce sherry, a blended wine. The *bodegas* of Gonzalez Byass and Pedro Domecq welcome visitors and there are festivities at the September vintage.

Cape St. Vincent, Cape Trafalgar . . . echoes of British naval victories prepare us for the massive Rock of Gibraltar, one of the classical Pillars of Hercules which guard the Mediterranean. Still a British colony, Gibraltar recently became accessible from Spain. At one time you had to cross from Algeciras to Tangier in Africa and take another boat back to the Rock.

Vines and olives of Andalucia yield to drifts of sugarcane as the road travels east to Malaga. Here begins another Spain, the kind foreign tourists know best: beaches and coastal walks, a backcloth of red rocks and evergreen shrubs. Torremolinos, Benidorm and Fuengirola are well patronized both summer and winter.

Malaga, a few miles inland, has excellent fish and seafood restaurants and a lopsided cathedral with wonderful 16th-century wood carving. But the jewel of this region is Granada in the foothills of Mulhacén (11,420 feet), Spain's highest mountain. The Spanish royal

15

Local color enriches Europe's favorite holiday island *right*. The tranquil life of the backstreets hardly suggests that an airport close by is handling more summer traffic than any airport in the United States. Such is the case with Palma, Majorca (also known as Mallorca), center of the Mediterranean's busiest holiday trade. Majorca is girdled with an unbroken chain of beaches, gulfs and inlets – some, like the bays of Palma and Pollensa, of vast extent. Many are developing fast and Palma itself, the capital, already has 300,000 inhabitants. But in the interior of Majorca, which is 60 miles long and 50 wide, there is still a good deal of unexplored country.

Bullfight at Palma de Majorca, Balearic Islands *above*. To Spaniards it is not a fight but a *corrida*, a 'running' of the bull. It is a drama which unfolds at its own pace, agreeable to rules and conventions which bewilder the uninitiated. Every sizable Spanish town has its *plaza de toros* (bullring) and the *corrida* takes place at least once a week, usually on Sunday evening, between March and October. As a spectator sport it is said to be losing its popularity, but the famous *toreros* still attract an enthusiastic following. Like fox-hunting in England, the bullfight may be morally indefensible; but it is too deeply rooted in the Spanish heritage to be seriously affected by the campaigns of abolitionists.

family, taking over the Alhambra (rose-red, built of clay), the Generalife (gardens) and the courts of the Moorish kings, in 1492, could not live up to such splendor and moved out again. The Moors were Moslems and there is still a small Moslem community in Spain.

Good-looking prosperous cities – Alicante, Valencia, and Tarragona with its cyclopean walls and Roman ruins – look eastward to the Balearics, a quartet of vacation islands 50 miles offshore. Majorca and Minorca, the largest, have been nominated the Mediterranean's most-visited islands – some achievement, when one considers the Greek and Italian competition.

Northwards stands Barcelona, a rectilinear city with fine avenues descending to the sea. One of them, Las Ramblas, is counted among Europe's great thoroughfares. Here the Catalan coast opens north and south on the scented woods and magnificent beaches of the Costa Brava and Costa Dorada – the Good Coast and the Gold Coast. Major resorts include Sitges, Tossa de Mar, Lloret de Mar, Llafranch and Rosas, but new ones continually arise. Most have a magnificent view of the Pyrenees, in whose heights nestles Andorra. Enthroned on high mountains, Andorra is a toy feudal domain of wild scenic beauty and duty-free shops, almost inaccessible in winter except to hardy skiers, and inclined to be congested in summer.

Sleepy time on a shady patio *above*. The former business routine of Spain – arrive at 11:00 am, stop for lunch at noon, take an afternoon-long siesta followed by a nap which lasts through early evening – is a thing of the past. But even in cities the energetic sightseer may have the streets to himself between 1:00 pm and 4:30 pm. By way of compensation, when the shops reopen they stay open until 8:00 pm or later and most evening entertainments begin when, in other parts of Europe, people are thinking of going to bed. It is common to find bars and restaurants humming merrily and full of customers at 4 o'clock in the morning.

Frills and flounces celebrate Moorish defeats *left*. In many a humble town of Spain, on a certain anniversary, you will see little knights in bedspreads, little Saracens in tablecloths ... they re-enact victory in a skirmish against the Moorish conquerors or the noble deeds of a local hero of long ago. These young ladies in their costumes will take part in street battles, with flowers, at the 'Christianos y Moros' fiesta (April 23rd and 24th) at Alcoy, north of Alicante.

The oldest resort on the Costa Brava *below*. Of all the little white towns which are strung like jewels round the brows of the Costa Brava's headlands, this one is probably the oldest. It had a fishmarket even before the Romans came, even before Hannibal passed through Spain with his elephants. The Moorish alcazabar is quite a recent addition: it was built in the 13th-century. This is Tossa de Mar, which pioneered holidays for foreign tourists. But visitors still have to share the beach with fisher folk painting their boats and mending their nets.

TRAVEL TIPS

Spain is one of Europe's largest states and regional distinctions are marked. No one is likely to speak much English. Country life moves at a mule's pace. Even Madrid shuts down for a three- or four-hour siesta.

Food in big towns and resorts is international. Spanish dishes most appealing to foreigners include *calamares* (squid), *gazpacho* (cold piquant vegetable soup) and *paella* (seafood with rice).

Bullfighting? The Spanish will tell you they prefer *futbol*. But every population center has its *plaza de toros* and from March to October, chiefly on Sunday evenings, the *corrida* draws big crowds.

Fairs and religious festivals are a way of life everywhere. Sunday, after mass, is a day of joyful activity. Dancing is both recreation and spectacle and the dances vary with the region.

The national currency, the *peseta*, has been several times devalued and Spain may be regarded as a cheap country in which to travel.

Rooftops of Cerdaña under the mighty Pyrenees *above*. Everyone talks of Gerona, millions pass through – and nobody stops there. It is the airport, specially built for tourist traffic, which serves the coastal playgrounds north of Barcelona. But Gerona and its neighboring village, Cerdaña, are picturesque places, clustered at the edge of foothills where the Ter and Oñar rivers break out of the mountains and head for the sea. Gerona cathedral is 800 years old; another church, reputedly built by Charlemagne, is 1000 years old. The 9000-foot crests of the Pyrenees look like they are toppling onto Cerdaña's roofs, but they are actually 50 miles away.

19

Gothic splendors carved from living rock. Where the main road leaves Normandy and enters Brittany, a minor route leads seaward and the astonishing prospect of the Mont St. Michel bursts into view. The original chapel (legend says) was built on the orders of the Archangel Michael himself. Then a Benedictine monastery was sculpted from the granite rock. At one period the place was deserted, at another it was a convict settlement. But as time went by the holy places were enlarged and beautified and a town grew up around them. A mile-long causeway connects Mont-St-Michel with the mainland.

FRANCE

Paris • Brittany • Normandy
Loire • Côte d'Azur • Savoy

French children learn the map of France by drawing a hexagon. Inhabitants of mainland France used to call themselves *hexagonistes*. The hexagon's six edges give the country six distinctive faces: the Channel coast, the Biscay coast, the Pyrenees, the Mediterranean coast, the Alpine regions and the northeastern lowlands – three maritime and three land frontiers. From Paris to the six corners, the roads and railways go out like spokes of a wheel.

Paris is the only really large city. France is a land of towns and villages, with broad tracts of undulating landscape comprising farms and hamlets, cornfields and an intensive viticulture. The six frontiers, almost wholly picturesque, enclose landscapes which the peculiar genius of the French (for wine, food, arts and crafts, intellectual activity, reason and good taste) has exploited. The vineyards of Burgundy and Bordeaux, the châteaux of the serpentine Loire, the walled towns of Languedoc, the Gothic spires of Chartres and Reims and belfries of Picardy, the stylish parterres of Versailles, Chantilly and Fontainebleau are only a few of the outstanding accomplishments. Abroad, the appeal of France is universal, for it is a country of great character, charm, and, above all, romance.

Paris is an easy city for novice travelers. First impressions are of contrast: broad boulevards and palatial buildings, mean streets and humble shops, elegant restaurants and sleazy dives. The tourist's Paris is grouped in a small space. With the latticed stanchions of the Eiffel Tower always in view, it is not possible to get lost as the apex, 985 feet above ground, is visible for 50 miles around.

A gentle stroll from the Arc de Triomphe, through the Tuileries Gardens and into the Place de la Concorde, takes in a good handful of the 'musts' of Paris. The route passes close to the Palais Royale with its three storys of antique shops and the Louvre, with its three universally known treasures: Venus de Milo, Winged Victory of Samothrace and Mona Lisa. (But the favorite gallery of modern art lovers is the Jeu de Paume, adjoining the Tuileries.)

Famous churches are prominent in the townscape, and offer magnificent viewpoints: Sacré Coeur's white dome, crowning the hump of Montmartre, early Gothic Notre-Dame and slender Sainte-Chapelle. Modern marvels of inspirational architecture are the Georges Pompidou Center, a cultural complex with ultra-modern features, the Montparnasse Tower, 56 storeys high, and Le Forum,

Notre-Dame of Paris: culmination of Gothic arts *left.* This site, on the Seine island called Ile de la Cité, was first occupied by pagan temples, then monkish cells, then the cathedral, founded 1163, where French kings and emperors were crowned. The glass-topped river boats carrying sightseers ply the Seine day and night, and Notre-Dame's huge rose window is a special attraction at sunset. Between quayside and cathedral runs a line of bookstalls and printstalls over which Parisians love to browse.

semi-subterranean and built in glass, a replacement for the old fruit and vegetable market of Les Halles.

Most imposing and historic of French châteaux, Versailles is 13 miles from the capital. Its gardens, illuminations and fountains (600 of them) impress the most jaded globetrotters. To the south stretch the forests and châteaux of Fontainebleau and Rambouillet, to the north the forest of St.-Germain-en-Laye, bristling with chestnut trees and old mansions.

Beyond Amiens, whose lofty cathedral is another jewel of Gothic inspirations, the industrial belt of Picardy stretches towards Belgium and the North Sea. Its towns bear the scars of World Wars I and II. Coastal towns, Calais, Boulogne and Dieppe, are chiefly noted as ferryports for England, but many small family resorts are strewn along the low cliffs, sand dunes and fine white sands of the shore. Le Touquet, with Trouville and Deauville farther west, were venues for the golf-and-gambling 'cocktail set' of the 1920s.

Inland, fertile Normandy's agricultural riches are harvested in meadows where there is always a solid town on the skyline, such as 'hundred-spired' Rouen, a monument to the enduring charms of medieval and Renaissance architecture. Along the coast are the wartime 'beaches' – Arromanches, Omaha and the rest.

Brittany pushes out her rocky peninsula 200 miles into the Atlantic. This is Celtic France, and the *dolmens* and *cromlechs* (prehistoric columns and circles), along with strange sounding place names, tell of a pagan society, predating the Romans, while other names, rock

The Pompidou Center: a glimpse of futurist Paris *below*. Conservative Parisians shrugged with Gallic resignation when they saw this block of glass and painted girders rising on the Seine's Right Bank. The structure, services and moving stairways are on the outside, leaving vast, uninterrupted exhibition spaces within. But Beaubourg, as the *cognoscenti* call it (full title: Centre National d'Art et de Culture Georges Pompidou) turned out to be a superb piece of modern architecture and an important adjunct to the capital's entertainment and cultural life. Exhibitions of arts, crafts and industrial design are held here. Concerts, plays and movies of the highest quality are presented. The plaza in front is reserved for clowns, acrobats, sword-swallowers, fire-eaters . . . for anyone with showbiz ambitions and a talent to amuse.

The Champs Elysées: the people's open-air salon *above*. Children play in the gardens by the Rond-Point while their parents window-shop. Visitors admire the Arc de Triomphe at one end and the Arc du Caroussel at the other (Napoleon's attempt to give central Paris monuments of antiquity like Rome). And everyone sits at some time or other at the famous pavement cafés, drinking coffee or Pernod and eating ice cream or pastries.

Market-garden produce in the stony streets of Paris *left*. Few vehicles, no police, hardly anyone in the quiet streets, a few stalls and wheelbarrows such as you might see in a country town . . . such were Montmartre and Montparnasse 150 years ago, according to the bohemians of the Latin Quarter. Early in the morning a few horse-drawn carts still rattle in from suburban market-gardens and the backstreets revert briefly to the street cries of long ago. Inhabitants descend to bargain for onions, garlic, eggplant and the herbs which differentiate the Parisian cuisine from others. The French housewife spends five hours a day in her kitchen, the American or British housewife between one and two.

Sacré-Coeur: lofty landmark on Paris's highest hill *left*. The pleasure seekers and kaleidoscopic strip lighting of Montmartre have taken over the lower slope of the Butte, highest of the seven hills of Paris; but the summit belongs – ironically – to the virgin-white dome of Sacré-Coeur, one of the three marvels of ecclesiastical architecture in the city (Notre-Dame and Sainte-Chapelle are the others). There is a splendid view from the dome, especially after dark when Paris is seen to be a true *ville lumière* (city of light). In the Montmartre cemetery are the graves of Alexander Dumas *fils*, Offenbach, Delibes, Berlioz, Zola and other 19th-century writers and artists who lived and worked in the shadow of Sacré-Coeur.

dwellings and the foundations of Mont St. Michel's island citadel, recall the early Christian saints. Dinard, St. Malo and La Baule are lively seaside resorts. The ancient river crossings, Dinan, Dol and Rennes, with thick walls and watergates, define some good touring country. Brittany has clean air, changeable skies, little towns of flinty pink and white stone ... and the Bretons themselves, farmers, fishers and lacemakers.

Southwards from the playgrounds of La Baule and Les Sables d'Olonne, the coast is flat and featureless but the inland towns, from Nantes to Tours, Orléans and Poitou, are soaked in history and dignified with Romanesque arts. On the River Loire, upstream from Nantes, begins the château route. The châteaux line the gravelly banks, even plant themselves firmly across tributaries. Chambord, Amboise, Chenonceaux, Blois, Azay-le-Rideau and many more are the fine flower of the French Renaissance, graphic evocations of an elegant and somber heritage.

South of the Gironde inlet, ribbons of sand reach down to Biarritz, St. Jean de Luz and similar long-established vacation grounds where the Pyrenees meet the sea. The low coastline, backed with *étangs*– reedy ponds – and pinewoods, is great camping country. The large port of Bordeaux, 60 miles from the sea, is a lesson in town planning: 15th-century tower gates, 18th-century opera house and town hall and more modern installations forming one harmonious complex. Bordeaux gives its name to the connoisseur's wines, which the British call claret – Mouton Rothschild, Château Latour and the rest. Sweet white Graves and Sauternes are also produced here.

Montmartre: a village of several mills, one of them red *above*. Hub of the garish side of Parisian entertainment, Montmartre could be described within living memory as a village with a little of everything, including pretty scenery and several mills, one of them red. Then the *Rat Mort*, haunt of Manet, Degas and Renoir, and the *Lapin Agile*, Picasso's favorite, started to encourage dancing to loud music under dim lighting. The 'Dead Rat' is dead and buried but the 'Active Rabbit' is still active as a *boîte* with cabaret and a tourist clientele. The old red mill burned down years ago, but an artificial windmill went up on the roof of the night club which they built on the site, and the *Moulin Rouge* has become a dazzling port of call on 'Paris by Night' tours.

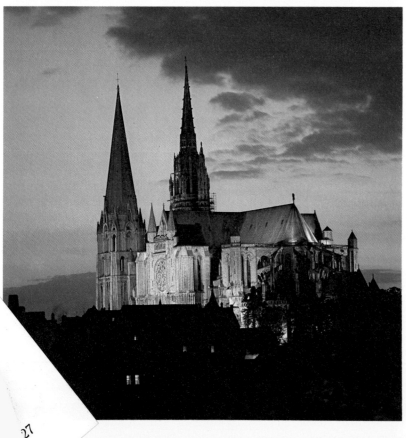

On the waterfront in dreamy Honfleur *above*. During the vacation period, when the yachts are in and the bars crowded, Honfleur is a cheerful place. Out of season it is a seaport the centuries have left behind. Here the River Seine, winding down from Paris and Rouen, reaches the sea. Honfleur's buildings date back to the 13th century; its 15th-century church, built by shipwrights, resembles an upturned boat. From its quays, in the 17th century, Champlain and other explorers set out to found French colonies in Canada and Louisiana.

Notre Dame de Chartres: the peak of ecclesiastical perfection *left*. Whoever called architecture 'frozen music' had probably just been to Chartres. Set in a landscape of fine cathedrals, about 50 miles south of Paris, it is the chief jewel in France's ecclesiastical crown. The wonders of Chartres unfold as you approach: first the great glittering rose window; then the rest of the medieval stained glass; finally the Royal Portal, where an unknown artist of the Middle Ages has depicted Christ triumphant with incomparable brilliance.

Inland roads wind lethargically among the clear streams of Dordogne, the rolling pastures of the Auvergne and the curious Massif Central, where conical hills have sprouted like mushrooms, thanks to primeval volcanic activity. Bordeaux to the Mediterranean is a picturesque trip by any route, and is landmarked by centers of outstanding beauty and interest: Périgord, truffle and *foie gras* country; Cahors, a castellated toytown; and Rocamadour, a place of pilgrimage, perched on an improbable crag. Other areas of interest include the amazing Stone Age caves of Lascaux with their colored drawings (chiefly of pregnant women); the Tarn gorges, 1500 feet down with multicolored strata; and the breezy uplands of the Cevennes, sprinkled with little spa towns.

The most southerly route, the Route des Pyrénées, follows that 200-mile mountain barrier from Atlantic to Mediterranean, tunneling through the forest, detouring now and again on road passes to Spain and giving access to places like Carcassonne, the supreme achievement of the military architect Viollet-le-Duc, and Perpignan, of Spanish character and beloved of artists.

We are now at the southernmost corner of France's 'hexagon,' the

A 'floating' château of the Loire
below. Built on a small lake in the Indre, tributary of the Loire, this agglomeration of spires, turrets and mullion windows is as romantic as its name: Azay-le-Rideau. The soaring, perfectly proportioned walls and blue slate gables give it a serene assurance, as though it were simply resting on the water like the swans which are often seen drifting around it. The interior is a museum of Renaissance furnishings and ornaments. The hotels and *auberges* of neighboring villages are charming too, and a few famous châteaux in this district of Indre-et-Loire have themselves become hotels.

Saint-Tropez: sophisticated outpost of the Azure Coast *above*. Strictly speaking, this small port does not belong to the French Riviera, which begins a few miles eastwards at Saint-Raphael. But the secluded beaches of Saint-Tropez and its neighbor Le Lavandou were the first to go topless – and then Brigitte Bardot decided to live in 'Saint-Trop'. Now the rich and famous as well as the bourgeoisie and the bohemians flock there as eagerly as to the beaches of Nice and Cannes, and the harbor is full of expensive yachts for most of the year. There are wonderful seascapes from the Citadelle, and the Annonciade museum on the quayside has an impressive modern art collection.

Vermilion Coast of the Roussillon province (both names refer to its rose-colored cliffs).

The Camargue country of the Rhône delta offers sluggish streams, rice fields, wild bulls and horses, egrets, flamingoes and ibises. It intervenes between the Côte Vermeille, with its international port of Marseille, and the Riviera or Côte d'Azur, France's principal vacationland. It was Europe's too, not long ago, and novels have dealt extensively with the good life in Bandol, St. Tropez, Cannes, Juan-les-Pins, Antibes and Nice, not to mention Monaco (Monte Carlo), the independent princedom and gambling mecca just short of the Italian frontier. These places nowadays have film festivals, jazz festivals and a mixed clientèle. The scented pinewoods, cork forests and glossy palmettoes are charming, the seascapes stupendous and the three tiers of *corniche* roads very exciting.

Nice to Paris, a venerable route which is now freeway, comes to the River Rhône at Avignon's celebrated bridge, a sad ruin today. This is Provence, a brown, scrubby, stone-walled and olive-clad country which has exercised its enchantment over the Romans (who left the amphitheater of Nîmes and the two-tiered Pont du Gard aqueduct behind) and over the artists Cézanne and Van Gogh, who painted scenes worthy of their genius around Arles and Aix-en-Provence. The latter place now holds a prestigious music festival in July and August.

Paris-bound, the historic highway sweeps through the Rhône valley by Montélimar, the famous nougat producing center, to the important commercial city of Lyon. Eastward the French Alps rear up and the mountain roads, the highest in Europe, lead to sophisticated ski resorts. Beyond Lyon, some rugged moorland shelters the Burgundy vineyards around Beaune, Macon and the Côte d'Or. The Burgundy canals offer a magical vineyard-banked trip; the canal-and-river routes through the Nivernais region provide a wonderfully tranquil one.

Dijon, former capital of the powerful Dukes of Burgundy, has a huge palace (the kitchens alone boast six fireplaces of staggering size), part of which is a museum of Burgundian history. Open-air theater is staged in the courtyard. This city is ideally placed for tours of the wine country and visits to Belfort and the Ballon d'Alsace (a steep hill, notorious in the bicycle Tour de France) above the German Rhine. Belfort commands the strategical gap between Jura and Vosges, two mountain ranges of forests and ravines. The Jura's limestone canyons, cut by the rapids of the Doubs river, are especially attractive. Northward again comes the formerly disputed territory of Alsace-Lorraine, more remarkable for battlefields and industry than for scenery.

The Côte d'Azur, where the only pursuit is pleasure *below*. Portrayed here is Roquebrune-Cap-Martin on the busiest and still perhaps most stunning of Europe's holiday coasts. The 50-mile-long French Riviera or Côte d'Azur is a gold and emerald ribbon pinned to sapphire bays and inlets. The adjectives are appropriate because in this happy land there appears to be no shortage of money and nothing to do but to enjoy oneself. The corniche roads wind through this coastline along their different ledges, offering sensational views. Napoleon built the Grande Corniche to accelerate the movements of troops but today it is a panoramic drive of twists and turns, with new visual enchantments at every bend.

Mont Blanc: the highest mountain in the Alps *above.* Italians claim that the summit of Mont Blanc (15,771 feet) is technically a few meters inside Italian territory. The French dispute it. Whichever it is, the Mont Blanc massif contains the highest peak in the Alps and the second highest in Europe; it is the most dramatic too, because of its needle-like pinnacles. The range has long been a challenge to mountaineers and from the beginning of time was an impassable barrier between northern and southern Europe. Since 1965 a seven-mile tunnel underneath Mont Blanc has been the means of a painless journey from France to Italy. Nearly two million vehicles pass through the tunnel every year. Some of the vehicles belong to skiers who take advantage of the excellent resorts on both sides of the tunnel and follow the best snow conditions.

Haute Savoie: provider of gastronomic riches *above.* Though much of the region is wild and steep and hard to cultivate, the industrious Savoyards have won gastronomic riches from the earth and from the goats, sheep and cattle that roam the upland pastures. Savoy cheeses, pictured here, make such epicurean dishes as *gruyères fondues* and *gratins dauphinois.* Evian mineral water from the banks of Lake Geneva is drunk the world over. Other delicacies from Savoy are *écrevisses* (crayfish) and *féra* (fish peculiar to Alpine lakes).

TRAVEL TIPS

Chauvin was an ardent admirer of Napoleon, and chauvinism, felt rather than expressed, is inherent in the French. A proud people (with much to be proud about), the French are also intelligent and passionate about food and style in general.

Provided the visitor does not spend too much time in Paris, this is not an expensive land in which to travel. Main roads are mostly freeways or fast toll roads. The express trains are the quickest in Europe. Food and drink are generally of good quality, but regional specialities are often costly. The *menu touristique*, which most eating places offer, ignores the delicacies and is good value. Coastal regions offer delicious fishy dishes, from the lobsters of Brittany to the anchovies of Provence and the pike of the northeast. Central and western France are the principal areas for suckling pig, goose liver, truffles, frogs' legs and snails. The northern regions cook in butter, the southern in olive oil. Judicious (but not fulsome) praise of French cuisine, as of antiquities, scenery and feminine chic, will make French hearts grow fonder.

When touring the vine-growing, wine-making regions of Burgundy or Bordeaux it should be possible for you to visit one of the châteaux. Telephone in advance the one you have selected to make sure your visit is possible and to make a booking.

Fontainebleau: 'the true abode of kings' *below*. The Emperor Napoleon called it the 'true abode of kings' and made it his home until his abdication in 1814. In front of that double curve of steps he bade his soldiers an emotional farewell, which is why the cobbled approach is called the Cour des Adieux. Fontainebleau is Italian in inspiration and style, the recreation of a small medieval palace by early 16th-century imported architects and craftsmen. It stands 30 miles south of Paris in its own forest, on the edge of which is the village which gave its name to the Barbizon school of 19th-century painting. The park is a popular walking, riding and picnicking area and the palace is open daily except Tuesdays to the public.

Cochem on the Moselle: a citadel among vineyards. The Moselle river (in German, Mosel) winds from Luxembourg to join the Rhine at Coblenz. The steep rounded hills on its banks are densely clothed in vineyards, interspersed with delightful river ports like Cochem.

GERMANY

Cologne • Black Forest • Heidelberg
Bamberg • Bavaria
Munich • Frankfurt • Berlin

U ntil the Iron Curtain fell, Germany was a big country in every sense. West Germany, officially the Bündesrepublik or Federal Republic, is still a big country and reaches from the Baltic Sea to the Alps. It is densely populated in most places. Since there are few natural boundaries, distances seem greater than they really are.

Some believe that if you take out the Rhine and the Black Forest nothing worth seeing is left. That is a superficial view of Germany. Rivers like the Neckar, Main, Isar and infant Danube exhibit antique towns and castles at every bend, just like the Rhine. The wildwoods of Harz, Spessart, Taunus and Eifel, largely of oak and beech, rival the Black Forest's conifers for beauty and majesty. Wide areas of West Germany are a credible homeland for the heroic sagas of Siegfried and the Valkyries and the cunning legends of Baron Münchausen, Till Eulenspiegel and the brothers Grimm.

East–West German relations steadily improve and the partition, despite pessimistic forecasts, has worked well. The former capital, Berlin, though deep in East German territory, is perfectly accessible. West Berlin is still the Federal Republic's largest city, but the civil servants are in Bonn and the major industries in Frankfurt, Stuttgart, Hamburg and along the lower Rhine.

A trip on the Rhine: the very idea makes the heart beat faster. Europe's most important waterway is most richly endowed with natural wonders . . . the question is, shall it be upstream or down? The answer is both, if possible. The big cruise boats do the round trip and there are also rail-and-cruise options.

Bonn, birthplace of Beethoven and now capital of West Germany but otherwise an undistinguished place, and Cologne a few miles away mark the limits of the downstream trip. Seaward from Cologne, where the Romans first built a bridge, the river is a corridor of commerce, thick with diesel-electric tugs towing endless trains of barges. Industry clusters at its banks – Düsseldorf, Duisburg, the Ruhr – but there are small towns of Dutch character too, which seem to have been lifted from a Breughel painting.

Fortunately, Cologne cathedral's delicate spires were untouched by war. There are older churches in the city: St. George's and St. Severin's

Cologne: Queen of the Rhine *left.*
Cologne is the largest Rhine city and, although 120 miles from the sea, its greatest river port. The city grew up at the lowest crossing-point, where the Romans first built a bridge. Despite suffering frightful damage during World War II, glories of medieval architecture still dominate the river banks and skyline and are well seen from the cable cars which cross the river. The huge cathedral of St. Peter and St. Mary (center of our picture) was begun in 1248 and finished 300 years later. Though not the biggest in Europe, as it was designed to be, it may well be the richest in stained glass. There is a shrine of particular extravagance and beauty, commemorating the three kings who paid homage to the infant Christ.

date from the 11th century. The city has several impressive museums, notably the Romano-German and the Prätorium.

Upstream from Cologne and Bonn the river flows through tourist Rhineland. Every waterside community has lively restaurants, hotels and wine centers. The river's course winds between the Taunus and Hunsrück ('Hound's Back') uplands, past Coblenz and Bingen and the rocky summits of Drachenfels and the mythical Lorelei. Where the Main and Moselle rivers come in, the Rhine is a sunny ornamental canal among vineyards arranged in formal patterns.

Larger towns like Mainz are confusing mixtures of medieval half-timbering and multi-story glass and concrete – as though the city fathers, asleep since 1300, had suddenly awakened and leaped ahead of the present day. Wiesbaden is a busy city and a graceful spa town.

At opposite ends of Wiesbaden's province, Hesse, Frankfurt and Kassel sustain the culture-clash theme. Theirs is the country of Grimms' fairytales, but they import Italian and African labor for their ultra-modern factories. In their satellite towns, automation and silicon-chip technology jostle the craft works and museums.

Vines and less glamorous plants – maize, potatoes, corn, fruits – are the constant companions of the middle Rhine. Above Karlsruhe and below Lake Constance, the river is a national frontier, shared with France and then Switzerland. Up to Schaffhausen's five cataracts it is navigable – and Schaffhausen is 600 miles from the sea.

The river near-misses Heidelberg. That time-worn town has a 14th-century university (the oldest in Germany) and is dramatically poised against castle rock and forested slopes. Southeastwards, the Neckar, one of Germany's most romantic rivers, tumbles down from the Black Forest.

Heidelberg: a setting for a student prince *above*. Some people, and not only the natives, consider Heidelberg the world's most beautiful city. Undeniably it has a most romantic setting above an exceedingly fine river, the Neckar, and some outstandingly handsome buildings. Heidelberg calls to mind alchemists, operetta (*The Student Prince*) and duelling scars. But the university, Germany's oldest, clearly kept tight control over eccentrics and hotheads – among claustrophobic bars and taverns stands the student jail to which offenders were unceremoniously dragged. The castle has an apothecary's museum and is a launching site for fireworks displays.

Bamberg: a town divided *right*. Bamberg is split by the two arms of the Regnitz river, which joins the Main a few miles further on. In ancient times one half of the place belonged to the bishops, the other half to the townspeople. So the splendid old Rathaus (Town Hall), from which both halves were governed, sits in midstream, equidistant from either side, and to cross the bridge you must walk through its rooms.

Neuschwanstein: Disneyland castle of a mad king *right*. Many a 'Beautiful Bavaria' picture book has this castle and the backdrop of its snow-water lake on the cover. King Ludwig II of Bavaria, an incurable romantic, indulged his dreams of a world peopled by gnomes, elves and heroes by constructing several costly follies. This one, close to the Austrian border near Füssen, was the most extraordinary. Ludwig reigned for 22 years (1864-86) before being declared insane (on the evidence of a disgruntled footman, it was said). He drowned himself in a lake. But during his reign he encouraged and financed Wagner, so perhaps he was not so mad after all.

Rüdesheim: a tourist mecca on the Rhine *below*. Rüdesheim is a cherished name on wine labels and a pleasant town of the Rheingau. The doorsteps of the houses are washed by picturesque reaches of the river. The narrow alleyway called Drosselgasse ('The Gullet'), leading from the landing stage to the main street, has become a gauntlet of pubs, wine bars and curio shops. At the top of the street are some interesting half-timbered houses built for rich merchants of long ago. Sekt, the Rhenish champagne, is made here.

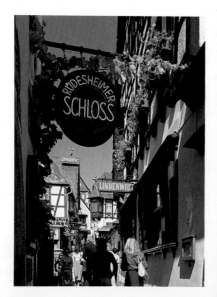

Munich: a million barrels of beer *below.* For 16 days, up to the first Sunday in October, the Hofbrauhaus (state brewery) and other companies set up their tents and gardens on the Theresienwiese near the Munich ringroad and a million Müncheners and visitors explode in a riot of merrymaking. This is the Oktoberfest. The city is awash with beer. The gargantuan capacity of drinkers is quite alarming. Amounts consumed, from the palest lagers to the darkest of syrupy 'heavies,' are scarcely less remarkable than the speed with which they are consumed. Close to a million kegs of beer are tapped at the Oktoberfest.

Munich: most German of German cities *above.* Sated as one may be with the Gothic magnificence of Germany, the eye lights up at the sight of this New Town Hall (the Old Town Hall is two blocks away), shining in all its glory after many vicissitudes. It was built only last century, rebuilt around 1906, destroyed in World War II and rebuilt again 1952–56. It has a Glockenspiel or musical clock, with mechanical figures. An elevator ascends to the 278-foot steeple, from which a wide expanse of Munich and the Isar valley can be seen. One of the twin cupolas of the Marienkirche or Frauenkirche is visible in the background of our picture. This too was destroyed in the war and meticulously restored.

They call it black because the density of foliage shuts out the sun. It is a continuation of the Vosges mountains of France. Above the treeline the rounded summits are bare, like the heads of tonsured monks. Beneath the trees the turf is soft and green.

Wherever they dug holes in the Black Forest, mineral water spurted out. Hence the profusion of towns, here and along the Rhine, prefixed '*bad*' (bath). Spa centers of Europe bow to Baden Baden, south of Karlsruhe. Like Wiesbaden, this was a Roman health resort. Generously wooded and furnished with lakes and walks around its Kursaal, Trinkhalle, Kurgarten and Kurhaus (casino), it conjures up visions of an imperial heyday. But Baden Baden is no sleepy museum-town. It is being replanned as a prestige conference center.

Munich: blotting paper for the liquor *right.* Although incredible quantities of beer are drunk at the Oktoberfest, more solid sustenance is not lacking. Whole oxen are roasted. Tons of ham and herring disappear down the throats of half a million customers and the German lard-cooked sausage comes into its own. Wherever a Munich brewer sets up his tent, a Munich baker lays out his stall. There are sweet pastries and savory pastries, white rolls and black rolls, sausage rolls and cheese rolls and even mustard rolls and horseradish rolls. This Oktoberfest stall holder specializes in pretzels of various shapes and sizes.

Frankfurt, where commerce and industry thrive *above*. Frankfurt on the River Main, quite close to the Rhine valley, is a visible manifestation of West Germany's post-war 'economic miracle.' In itself it is not an important tourist town, but admirers of the domestic architecture of the Middle Ages will find charming old houses, sensitively rebuilt or restored, in the Old Town. A scale model of the Old Town, in fine detail, is exhibited at the city museum, next to the 13th-century Nikolaikirche in our picture. On the right of the church the trio of gable-ends (an unofficial trademark of Frankfurt) identifies the building called Römer, the old-time City Hall.

West Berlin: metropolis in exile *right*. West Berlin has all the equipment of a capital city except Government ministries and state apparatus. It maintains a rich cultural and leisure life with theaters and nightclubs, festivals of films, fashion and jazz, and deluxe hotels which were built to fill the gaps left by wartime bombing. The world's principal airlines (but not Lufthansa) fly into Berlin, and the U-Bahn (subway) system provides fast trains all over the city. Our picture, taken from the Europa Center, looks out on the modernistic Kaiser Wilhelm Memorial church and down the Kurfürstendamm, once a street of elegant shops.

Bavaria's chief town is Munich, a rich city, regarded as Germany's chief cultural metropolis and the capital of beer making and beer drinking. The Munich Oktoberfest is known the world over.

Two fascinating Bavarian towns towards the Czech and East German frontiers are Regensburg and Nürnberg (the Nuremberg of *The Mastersingers* and of Hitler's mass rallies).

West Berlin, 100 miles inside East Germany, is accessible by road or rail from Hanover and Hamburg and by air from several European capitals. An excursion to East Berlin (you simply show your passport and pay two dollars at Checkpoint Charlie on the famous Wall) is always a good talking point.

TRAVEL TIPS

The Germans themselves are indefatigable travelers, and are ordinarily fair, honest and helpful to the stranger within their gates. They are a well-educated, if sometimes pedantic, people.

Food tends to be heavy. Sausages of various kinds are ubiquitous, rich desserts a feature of every menu.

Communications are first class. In all public places a high value is set on hygiene: the cheapest guesthouse or café is spotless.

Under the Grand St. Bernard. To the Swiss the 'alps' are not the mountain peaks which divide Switzerland from France, Italy and Austria, but the high pastures beneath them – like these slopes of Pallasuit. In summer, grass and cereals are harvested for cattle fodder and the tinkle of cow-bells is heard. In winter it's a different story!

— SWITZERLAND —

Geneva • Zurich
Bern

Switzerland is small – not much bigger than Vermont – but it's scenery is astonishing in its diversity. The Alpine chain is its greatest feature and is the source of two great European rivers, the Rhine and the Rhône.

Though landlocked in the heart of Europe, the country has escaped Europe's stormy history and has been an independent federation of 'cantons' since 1291 – the era of William Tell. Famed for its financial institutions, its quality food products (especially cheeses and chocolates) and its precision engineering (clocks and watches), this archetypal neutral state is the headquarters of world peace conferences and international humanitarian organizations.

From the west, hill-passes of the Jura mountains lead to Geneva, one of the smartest and cleanest cities on earth. The world's tallest fountain-jet (500 feet) spurts from Lake Geneva, known locally as Lac Léman. Charming towns cluster along the lakeside roads. Southward, impressive routes leading to Italy climb into the Alps. Alternatively, you may drive through the Mont Blanc tunnel to Italy, or put your automobile on the train.

Needle-peak of the Central Alps *right.* The Matterhorn's pyramidical summit, rising abruptly from the highlands of Valais to 14,780 feet, defied mountaineers until about a century ago. Nowadays, if you conquer the peak you may well find a picnic party on top. From the snow-water lake called Riffelsee (foreground of picture), glacial valleys descend to the busy ski centre of Zermatt and the infant river Rhône, whose glacier (with pedestrian underpass) is a great tourist attraction.

City of the Bear *below.* The Swiss federal capital, Bern, a compact little city of arcaded streets, quaint buildings and flowery parks, is known as the 'City of the Bear' – with live bears in the Bärengraben and fantastically decorated bear statues in public places. At the famous 12th-century Clock Tower (background of picture) mechanical figures, including bears, perform every hour.

Treasuries of rustic arts *below.*
Gaunt-looking chalets, like this one, in the Romansch-speaking regions of the Grisons (in the eastern Alps), are steep-pitched against snow and emblazoned with baroque decorations.

Europe's winter playground *bottom.*
Skiing for pleasure came relatively recently to Switzerland. 'Where are you taking those planks to?' asked the Grindelwald station master of the first British ski party around 1880. But within two generations humble villages like Zermatt, Davos and St. Moritz had become sophisticated resorts, and the Swiss Alps were synonymous with winter sports.

Sherlock Holmes' fans make for Meiringen (scene of his last encounter with his enemy Professor Moriarty), which is near scenic Interlaken and within walking distance of the Reichenbach Falls. Painless mountaineering can be done on a fine mountain railroad from Grindelwald, across the Eiger's north face to the summit of the Jungfrau at 13,468 feet. Eastward, among the peaks and valleys of the Grisons, lie the pioneer winter-sports grounds of Davos, Klosters and St. Moritz. South across the Alps is Italian-speaking Switzerland, with the lake resorts of Locarno and Lugano.

Head north towards Germany for commercial and industrial Switzerland: Zurich the biggest city and banking capital; Lucerne, romantic birthplace of Swiss independence; and Schaffhausen and Basel, notable river ports. Delightful return routes to Geneva cross the undulating Vernese Oberland and the Vaud, sprinkled with aristocratic old towns like Murten, Fribourg and Gruyère. Neuchâtel, a stately city with some fascinating museums, stands by the broad lake to which it gives its name.

TRAVEL TIPS

D. H. Lawrence condemned the 'average ordinariness' of the Swiss, but their neatness and passion for hygiene in shops, hotels and restaurants are most welcome to tourists. They are multilingual – French, German, Italian and English are generally understood. The railroad is excellent, and gasoline is relatively inexpensive.

Ullsfjord: 50 miles of Arctic serenity. This fjord is one of the least accessible in northern Norway, but on the far side of its isthmus stands Tromsö, 'capital of the Arctic,' with bus tours and cable cars providing views over the surrounding district.

— SCANDINAVIA —

Denmark
Sweden • Norway

All of Scandinavia is a vacation resort with the emphasis on fresh air and healthy outdoor activities ... and grand scenery. Denmark is split into islands, some large with well-groomed countrysides and riviera coastlines, others tiny and tranquil. Copenhagen, the capital, is a tolerant, civilized city of notable charm, entirely surrounded by sea. Sweden offers a bewildering spread of big lakes and small rivers and, in the north where reindeer roam, an exciting wilderness of forested mountains. Its capital, Stockholm, called the Venice of the North for its waterways and the Paris of the North for its fashionable shops, is a splendid combination of medieval and modern architecture. Norway, land of the midnight sun, has mountains and plateaus where skiing is both a sport and a way of life. It has a superbly romantic rocky coastline, through which fishing craft and cruise ships find passages via silent, crystal-clear fjords, to sequestered harbors far inland.
Historically, the kingdoms of Denmark, Sweden and Norway are inextricably mixed up, but each has preserved its identity. All three are socially progressive countries which have adopted many innovative reforms.

Denmark consists of the tapering peninsula called Jutland (attached to Germany), several islands, principally Funen, Sealand, Langeland, Lolland and Falster, and hundreds of tiny islets. All this adds up to an ideal vacation country for all ages.

Copenhagen stands off-center, two islands removed from the mainland of Jutland. From a tower block in downtown Copenhagen you see a lot of Sweden across the bright sea channel, but not much of Denmark.

It is a bewitching city. It contains the dignified palaces of Christiansborg, now the seat of government, and Amalienborg, home of the Danish royal family – a democratic dynasty which never held itself aloof from the people. A third city-center palace, Rosenborg, in a public park inhabited by swans, ducklings and seasonal drifts of semi-wild flowers, is a Renaissance gem.

In Strøget (it means 'strolling'), Copenhagen has one of Europe's famous shopping thoroughfares, an all-pedestrian route made of five consecutive streets leading from dockland to city square. On Strøget you find smart shops and ancient dusty boutiques selling china, glassware, silver, rare prints and antiques. There are scores of coffee bars, salad bars and restaurants.

The Little Mermaid, pensive on her rock *left.* Designed to illustrate a fairytale and pay tribute to its author, Hans Christian Andersen, the Little Mermaid has become a symbol of Copenhagen. Her rock is on the Langelinie promenade in the Danish capital's northern suburbs, a few yards from the shore. But not far enough, for she has proved vulnerable to souvenir hunters and now, understandably, her expression is one of despondency. Across the channel is Copenhagen's island suburb, Christianshavn, with commericial and naval dockyards.

Denmark: peasant simplicity of times past *left*. Denmark's numerous islands once vied with each other in the neatness and harmony of their peasant costumes. Almost every item of clothing had a story attached to it and the whole ensemble was a picture of restrained elegance. Nowadays the costumes are seen only on special occasions. A magnificent collection of them is vividly displayed in the open air in the folk-dancing events at the Frilands museum at Lyngby on the northern outskirts of Copenhagen.

Elsewhere, traffic flows smoothly on broad avenues which terminate in cobbled byways, little bridges and canals. The *al fresco* excursion boats come and go. Boat tours are good value.

Tivoli gardens in the city's heart are a unique attraction. In a well-behaved way they recreate the pleasure gardens of 18th-century London. There is something for everyone: beautifully appointed restaurants, theaters, concert halls, pagodas, lakes, artist-designed flower-beds and illuminations. But the most abiding of countless warm memories of Copenhagen must be the all-pervading friendliness and cheerfulness in those immaculate shops and restaurants.

The Danish 'mainland' is a showplace of Gothic and Renaissance castles and manor houses, of which Spøttrup, Sønderborg, Skaføgaard and Clausholm are typical.

The ripe old buildings of Aarhus, second city of Denmark, and the schnapps-and-oysters northern 'capital' of Aalborg, on its labyrinthine fjord are among the best sights in Jutland. Others include the lakeland of Silkeborg, where Sky Mountain (highest hill in Denmark) soars to all of 500 feet, and the many charming coastal and lagoon villages with wide-open strands. The most astonishing place must be the 'kingdom' of Legoland, near Billund airport. Exhibition halls trace the history of this Danish constructional toy.

Great bridges link Jutland with Funen, island of Hans Christian Andersen. He is the national hero and the kindly influence of his life

Historic waterfront of a seagirt city

below. Tato Jack ... Cap Horn bar ... the names of the canalside taverns, tattooists and ship chandlers of old Copenhagen persist, but it is mostly make-believe. The former squalid dives are coffee bars, the tall ships are floating restaurants and the high narrow buildings are topped by penthouse apartments for which the city's professional classes pay exorbitant rents. From Nyhavn, shown here, open-topped excursion boats probe the nooks and crannies of the canals in a fascinating tourist trip.

and work permeates many aspects of Danish society. The birthplace museum at Odense has movies, memorabilia and a whole library of *Andersen's Fairy Tales* in many languages.

Swift vessels connect Funen with Sealand (the island of Copenhagen), and with Kronborg the sturdy sea-fortress which Shakespeare called Elsinore.

These main islands are Europe's larder: fatstock for Germany, butter and bacon for Great Britain. Their coasts are ringed with delightful fishing villages and low-beamed inns. There, and at diminutive ports in islets like Bornholm, Samsø, Aerø, Anholt and Laesø, and islets tinier still, like sandbanks in the sea, small-boat sailors and the bucket-and-spade brigade settle in for a vacation.

Military needs dictated the site of Sweden's capital, Stockholm, where a lake disgorged into the Baltic Sea. Bays, inlets, bridges and island forts make Stockholm look like a city afloat. Terrace views from

Queen of the Baltic in her winter dress
left. Wrapped in snow, Stockholm, the 'Queen of the Baltic', looks regal indeed. Winter brings out the best in the solid stone and red brick, the open belfries of the oldest churches, the slim spires and tall narrow windows. This is a community confined by lakes and channels; the white excursion steamers are camouflaged against floating lumps of ice. In a hard winter the waters of Stockholm are frozen, which makes problems for her many swans and also for city transport, since many goods and passengers are carried by water. Waterfowl converge on Mälarstrand, expecting to be fed.

Stockholm: in the depths of the Old Town *above.* Stockholm has undergone a great deal of replanning and reconstruction both in the suburbs and in the heart of the city. But much of the section called the Old Town really is old, with some authentically antiquated buildings. Lanes like Gåsgränd, shown here, wander through archways and among medieval tenements and postage-stamp squares. One *gränd* (lane) hereabouts, the Marten Trotzigsgränd, with house numbers and street lighting, is believed to be the narrowest thoroughfare in Europe; it is about three feet wide.

'Advance, friend, and be recognized.' *left.* Ferocious appearance and *pickelhaube* (spiked helmet) notwithstanding, the sentry at Stockholm's Royal Palace allows everyone to pass without question, even when the Royal Family is in residence. The Palace has 550 rooms, so there is space for all. Visitors are permitted to inspect the Treasury, which houses the Swedish crown jewels, and the Hall of State, where the King's silver throne stands.

Skansen: a microcosm of Swedish life and work *above*. There is no need to voyage to the northern coastlands to search for quaint old houses roofed with turf or seaweed. They can be seen in Stockholm at the park called Skansen – uplifted, transported and re-erected along with other regional curiosities from all parts of Sweden. Apart from its open-air folk museum (the first in the world, established 1891), Skansen has a zoo, craftshops, restaurants and elaborate gardens. It is half-an-hour's walk from the city center – a popular Sunday afternoon stroll – and may also be reached by bus or ferryboat.

Little seaports lost from the world *right*. From the heights above a Lofoten fjord the scene suggests a toy village of Legoland . . . but this is real life among the islands which form a protective barrier for the northern Norwegian coast against Arctic gales. The fishing villages cling to the islands' edges as precariously as seabirds' nests. Coastal steamers from Bodø to Tromsö and North Cape negotiate the intricate channels of the Lofotens under sharp steep cliffs and pay calls on thriving communities whose existence is not suspected until the last rocky promontory draws back suddenly like a curtain.

Djurgaards or The Strand suggest a juvenile population: flowery playparks, boating ponds and paddling pools. Generations of city fathers (a 'Beauty Council' controls development) have ensured that the Queen of the Baltic remains serene, tidy and good looking. The large island of Djurgaarden supports Stockholm's main cultural complex, which includes the big Liljevalch and Thielska galleries, zoo and folk park of Skansen, the Nordiska Museum of Swedish crafts history . . . and the amazing *Wasa*, salvaged and dried out, the warship which wasted Sweden's treasury and sank as soon as she embarked on her maiden voyage in 1628.

In the Old Town, between the two main bridges, stands the Royal Palace, open to all, and the Great Church, dating from the mid-1200s. Lanes of little shops and slim medieval tenements contrast with the modern City Hall and its triple-crowned tower on the lake shore near Central Bridge. Fine large concert halls and a leading European opera house confirm Sweden's prominence in music and drama. In the Concert Hall, on Kungsgatan, the Nobel prizes are awarded. On Lovön island, a short taxi ride or 20-minute boat trip from City Hall, is the

elegant 17th-century palace of Drottningholm, a Swedish Versailles.

Many visitors arrive in Sweden at Malmö, a rifle-shot from Copenhagen, or Hälsingborg, a stone's throw from Hamlet's castle at Helsingør, or at the large port of Göteborg, which offers an idyllic three-day canal trip to Stockholm. From Norrköping, south of Stockholm, or from Göteborg, interesting routes wind through Sweden's lake district. (Vänern is the largest lake in Europe.) From Kalmar, farther south, ferryboats sail to the nearby island of Oland and to uniquely atmospheric Visby, clasped in its girdle of stout walls, on Gotland.

North from Stockholm, beyond historic Uppsala with its Gothic castle, cathedral and university, is the Dalarna region, Sweden's smiling heart of birchwoods, folksy villages and lakes. Increasingly wild and romantic country with a prolific wildlife leads on to a Swedish Lappland, where winter frosts turn the ground to iron. But even among the simplest villages, complex hydro-electric stations and electronically operated canal locks are found.

Northward still, into the Finnmark region of Norway, roads lead to Hammerfest, at 72 degrees lattitude the northernmost city in the world. Its ravaged hills are viewpoints for the midnight sun (early June to mid-July). Passenger ships go on to Honningsvaag, where a bus departs for the observation hall at North Cape, Europe's most northerly headland.

From Kirkenes on the Soviet frontier the Arctic Highway winds west and south around the fjords, all the way to Trondheim, 1000 miles away – a typical Norwegian road, skillfully engineered. Views of the fjords stamp themselves indelibly on the memory, where 6000-foot ridges stop short on the sea's edge and drop almost perpendicularly, to be mirrored at great depths in the water. A lifetime is too short to explore all the fjords, but Hardanger, Sogne (110 miles long) and Romsdal, all south of Trondheim, should not be missed. Of numerous towns with antique, often exotic, wooden buildings of large size and character, Bergen is especially handsome. From Bergen the botanical wilderness of the Telemark valley and the panoramic Hardanger plateau route lead to Oslo, the capital. The most popular winter sports centers are along these trails.

The scale of Oslo's natural harbor is a revelation and there are many historic buildings. Over the centuries, unhappily, fires have destroyed many more. In the capital city's entertainment life, drama is paramount, as befits Ibsen's homeland. Apart from the National Theater there are numerous 'little' and experimental theaters and several theaters exclusively for children. Oslo's museums tell the story of polar, exploration, a Norwegian tradition. Everyone goes to see Thor Heyerdahl's Kon-tiki raft, which has a museum to itself. There is yachting in the fjord and skiing on the suburban hills.

Geirangerfjord: a sea-filled Grand Canyon *left*. The complicated network of fjords which run inland from the Norwegian coast south of Alesund present what some consider the most sensational visual experience in all the fjord country. The sea, penetrating the recesses of mountainland called Romsdal, and growing ever calmer and more mysterious, becomes a riverine lake, then a canal, then the narrowest of channels under canyon walls of rock. Geirangerfjord and Nordfjord are the deepest and longest inlets, and the skyline drive from the head of one to the head of the other climbs over the 5000-foot 'roof' of Norway, with unforgettable views of the fjords.

TRAVEL TIPS

Scandinavia promotes democratic rights, sexual equality, social care and higher education. These lands are particularly agreeable for their civilized customs, care for the environment and high standards of hygiene. Accommodation at all levels is satisfactory. Transport services are remarkably efficient and comprehensive.

Norway and Sweden are reputedly expensive countries – they were, but are growing more reasonable. Swedes and Norwegians regard Denmark as quite inexpensive already. Shopping hours are similar to those of America and Britain, though flexible – not to say capricious – in remote localities. Banks close at 4:00 pm (in Sweden 6:00 pm) and remain closed in Norway and Sweden on Saturdays.

Danish *smorrebrød* and Swedish *smörgåsbord*, open sandwiches, are world renowned. Breakfasts, normally included in hotel overnight prices, are serve-yourself meals with Danish pastries a speciality. At other meals trout, salmon, lobster, crab and shrimps regularly appear. Reindeer, sweeter and firmer than venison, is eaten in northern Norway and Sweden. Most Scandinavians love chocolate and ice cream desserts. They consume more coffee, per capita, than any other nation.

Alcoholic drinks are the apéritif-type schnapps (very cheap), imported wines (fairly costly), and spirits (very costly). Denmark serves liquor at all hours, Norway and Sweden not before lunchtime, and never on Sundays. Drinking and driving in Scandinavia is a serious offense. Tipping in Norway and Sweden is covered by a service charge. In Denmark, tipping is forbidden by law.

Lappland: a life in the Arctic wilderness *below*. The Lapps are a race without a country but they can claim to be at home all over northern Scandinavia, from the USSR to Finland, and from Sweden to Norway. They are nomadic and spend their lives in restless pursuit of the migratory reindeer. Most of their possessions – tents, clothes, implements – are fashioned from the skins, antlers and bones of those creatures. Unlike the Eskimos, they are dour, introverted people who tend to avoid tourists. Life grows no easier for them: it is estimated that there are fewer than 40,000 left. There is a Lapp museum at Jokkmökk on the Arctic circle in Swedish Lappland.

The Otertindan: homeland of the trolls *right*. The high plateaus, lakes and peaks which form the backbone of the Scandinavian peninsula are the misty land of the trolls and subterranean spirits of Norwegian folklore. Some roads are closed by snow between October and early June (although automobiles can be carried by rail on major routes). But cross-country motoring is always an experience and the reward, near the end of the trip, is an eagle's-eye view of the ribbon of fjords to which you are to descend. The sharp cones in our picture are the Otertindan mountains, 4460 feet high. They are north of Narvik. Somewhere here, one feels, must be the entrance to the Hall of the Mountain King.

Index

Acknowledgements

The publishers thank the following for providing the photographs in this book:
The Photo Source/CLI 4/5, 6/7, 11, 12, 15, 17, 18 below, 19, 25 below, 26, 29, 32 below, 44, 46/7, 54, 56, 57 below, 58, 62; Zefa 1, 2/3, 8/9, 10, 13, 14, 16, 18 above, 20/21, 22/23, 24, 25 above, 27, 28, 28–29, 30, 31, 32 above, 33, 34/35, 36/37, 38, 39, 40, 40/41, 42, 42/43, 43, 44/45, 45, 48, 49, 50/51, 52/53, 54/55, 57 above, 58/59, 60/61, 63.